Editor
Lorin E. Klistoff, M.A.

Editor in Chief
Ina Massler Levin, M.A.

Illustrator
Alexandra Artigas

Cover Artist
Denise Bauer

Creative Director
Karen J. Goldfluss, M.S. Ed.

Art Coordinator
Renée Christine Yates

Imaging
James Edward Grace

Publisher
Mary D. Smith, M.S. Ed.

Author

Penny Carter

The classroom teacher may reproduce copies of materials in this book for classroom use only. Reproduction of any part for an entire school or school system is strictly prohibited. No part of this publication may be transmitted, stored, or recorded in any form without written permission from the publisher.

Teacher Created Resources, Inc.
6421 Industry Way
www, CA 92683
www.teachercreated.com

ISBN: 978-1-4206-8978-5

© 2009 Teacher Created Resources, Inc.
Made in U.S.A.

Teacher Created Resources

Table of Contents

Introduction

Using poetry with children is a wonderful way to instruct and motivate them. In this book, word families are presented through the use of motivating poems. A word family is a group of words sharing a common phonetic element. Children learn that words often contain these recognizable chunks. The cracking of this code provides predictable patterns and is a help in decoding new words. With practice, children learn to use these chunks instead of sounding out one letter at a time. Decoding takes place more quickly and efficiently.

The poems in this workbook can be presented in different ways depending on the age and ability level of the children. For younger children, the poems can be read together as a class. The teacher can guide the children through the process of listening for and locating word families. Older children can utilize the sounds to decipher words on their own.

Before each new word family is presented, prepare a copy of the appropriate poem for each child. Read through the poem first and carry on a discussion making sure the children comprehend the message of the poem. Then have the children highlight the words containing the word families.

Each poem in this workbook is followed by one or two worksheets. Some are suitable for the younger primary child, while the others are designed for children who are more advanced. These worksheets are an effective way to provide differentiation for a class of students of varying ability levels. Using this book will promote overall literacy skills. Besides reading practice, the use of this book provides opportunities for spelling lessons and writing practice. Some of the poems have connections to social studies and science.

The teacher may decide to have the children take the poems home to practice, or it may be preferable that the children save their poems to become part of a poetry collection. A CD is also included. Color transparencies or black and white copies of the poems can be made.

CORRELATION OF STANDARDS

Standard: Uses the general skills and strategies of the reading process

- Creates mental images from pictures and print
- Uses basic elements of phonetic analysis to decode unknown words
- Reads aloud familiar stories, poems, and passages with fluency and expression

Standard: Uses reading skills and strategies to understand and interpret a variety of literary texts

- Uses reading skills and strategies to understand a variety of familiar literary passages and texts (e.g., poems)

Standard: Uses listening and speaking strategies for different purposes

- Recites and responds to familiar stories, poems, and rhymes with patterns

---

All standards listed above are from A Compendium of Standards and Benchmarks for K–12 Education (Copyright 2004 McREL, www.mcrel.org/standards-benchmarks) Language Arts (Grades K–2).

Come Back, Quack!

Zack, the duck, woke up one day
To find his quack had gone away.

He knew he had to get it back.
He packed some snacks in his knapsack.

He walked along the railroad track.
He heard a whistle, not his quack.

Then in the woods he heard whack, whack;
But it was just a lumberjack.

Soon he came to a run-down shack.
He looked in back by a tall haystack.

Alas, his quack was not around,
But he found Mack, the old bloodhound.

Mack said, "Your quack will be revealed."
His nose led them to a football field.

That's where they found Zack's brother Quack,
Who was the team's star quarterback.

Name: _____ **Date:** _____

A. Quack, the quarterback, can only throw footballs with letters that make a word when *–ack* is added. Write the letter(s) to make *–ack* family words in the boxes below the footballs. Color the footballs that Mack can throw.

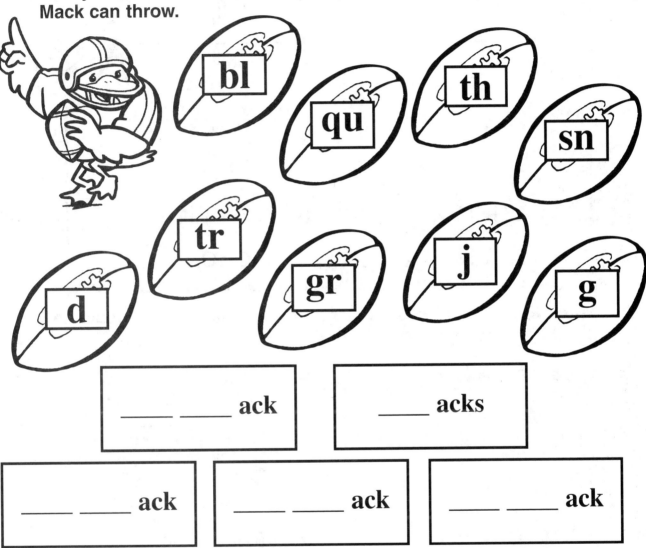

B. Fill in the blanks with an *–ack* family word above that makes sense.

1. A train runs on a railroad _____ .

2. When I am hungry, I eat a _____ .

3. The sound a duck makes is _____ .

4. The sky at night is the color _____ .

5. In the gym we do some jumping _____ .

Name: _____ **Date:** _____

A. In the poem, Zack searched for his brother Quack. Now it is your turn to do some searching. Match each word part with an *–ack* family word to make a compound word.

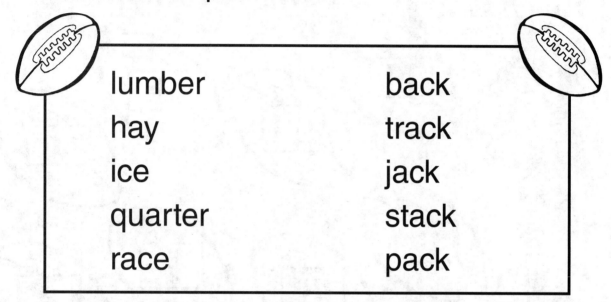

lumber	back
hay	track
ice	jack
quarter	stack
race	pack

B. Write "yes" or "no" to tell whether the following things could be found or heard on a football field.

1. quarterback

_____

2. haystack

_____

3. icepack

_____

4. shack

_____

5. fullback

_____

6. feedback

_____

7. flapjack

_____

8. whack

_____

9. racetrack

_____

10. quack

_____

Off to the Mall

Mom called to me, "It's time to shop.
Your shoes are way too small."
I tried to stall her, "Please, Mom, no!
I really hate the mall!"

Inside the mall so big and tall
Sat a gumball machine.
My mother used up all her change.
I only wanted green.

Then next I saw the choo-choo train,
I knew I had to ride.
I jumped the wall and climbed aboard.
My mom was horrified!

I saw the lights in the arcade,
I begged to play pinball.
Then mother said, "That's all, let's go.
I really hate the mall!"

Name: _____ Date: _____

A. **Color the gumballs that make *–all* family words.**

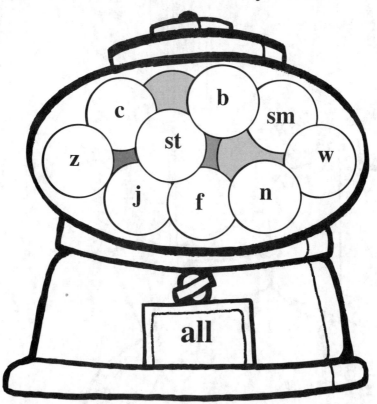

B. **Use *–all* family words to complete the rhymes below.**

Call	fall	small	ball	mall

1. Come one, come all,
   There's a sale at the _____ .

2. _____ your pals to let them know.
   It's more fun than a picture show.

3. In the toy store choose a ball.
   Some are big and some are _____ .

4. There's a lot to see at the mall.
   Watch your step so you don't _____ .

5. It's time to leave for it's nightfall.
   But it's okay, we had a _____ .

Happy as a Clam

Once there was a sad, little clam
That lived in a lake near Birmingham.

She sat and watched the fish that swam,
This tiny clam whose name was Pam.

Pam wished to swim just like the fish
With a graceful tail that went swish, swish.

She studied for a swim exam,
So many strokes, she tried to cram.

A friendly fish whose name was Sam
Reminded her she was a clam.

Just then a piranha happened by
Searching for tasty treats to try.

"Oh, dear," they thought. "We're in a jam."
Wham! Pam's shell slammed, and Sam did scram.

Poor Sam swam fast, but he was caught.
"I'm glad I am a clam," Pam thought.

Name: _____ **Date:** _____

A. **Find and list the *–am* word family words in the poem "Happy as a Clam." Use each one only once. Practice reading the words.**

1. _____   7. _____

2. _____   8. _____

3. _____   9. _____

4. _____   10. _____

5. _____   11. _____

6. _____   12. _____

B. **Color the clams that make *–am* family words. Cross out the clams that are nonsense words.**

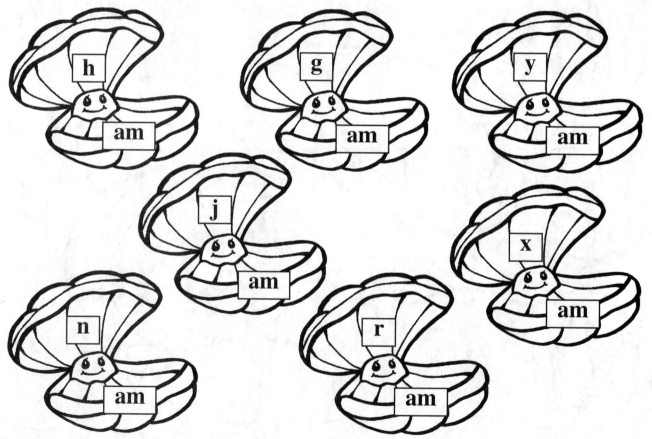

Name: _____ **Date:** _____

A. In the poem "Happy as a Clam," Pam and Sam find themselves in a jam. Fill in the missing words found in the word box to help tell the story of a baseball pitcher who found himself in trouble.

clammy	jam	slam	scram	Wham

I love pitching, but one particular day that was not

the case. I found myself in a real _____ . The

score was tied. The bases were loaded. The batter

coming up could really _____ the ball. My

hands were starting to feel _____ . I threw

the pitch. _____ ! I heard the bat and ball

connect. It was a pop fly. The third baseman had to

_____ to get the ball. "Out!" the umpire

shouted. I was thrilled!

B. Tell about a time that you were in a jam. How did you get out of it?

_____

_____

_____

_____

_____

A Goldfish Named Frank

A goldfish named Frank
Lived in a huge tank.
When children would visit,
His poor fishy heart sank.

They'd point to the others.
Those fish would be yanked.
But sad little Frank,
His hopes slowly shrank.

Then Frank decided
He needed a prank.
He began swimming backwards
The length of the tank.

"I want that cool stunt fish,"
Cried Hank, a young lad.
"Oh, thank you," bubbled Frank.
He was no longer sad.

Name: _____   **Date:** _____

A. **Circle the goldfish that are members of the *–ank* word family and belong in the tank. Practice reading the words.**

B. **Fill in the blanks with the *–ank* word family goldfish that are circled.**

1. Hank bought Frank with money from his piggy _____ .

2. Hank put Frank in a new _____ .

3. Hank put in some shells that _____ to the bottom.

4. As shells fell into the tank, I heard them _____ .

5. Frank liked his new tank. He looked at Hank and seemed to say, " _____ you."

Name: _____ **Date:** _____

A. Color the bubbles that would make a word when added to –ank.

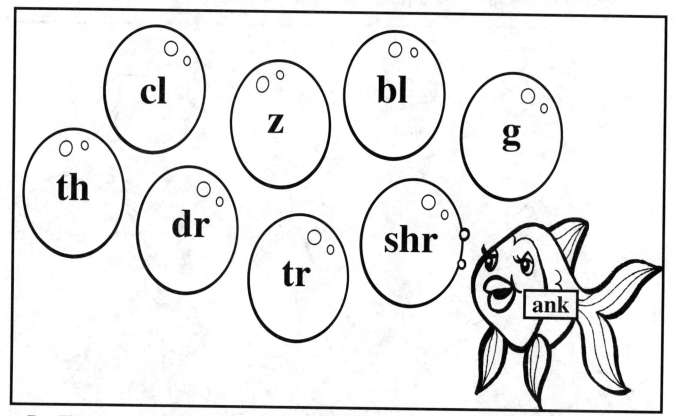

B. Fill in the blanks with an –ank family word.

blank	yank	cranky	outranks	plank

1. On a pirate ship, someone might be told to walk the
   _____ .

2. If you can't remember an answer, you might say, "I've
   drawn a _____ ."

3. On a boat the captain is in charge. He _____
   the crew.

4. You know that you've caught a fish when you feel a
   _____ on the line.

5. If you have fished for a long time and have not caught any
   fish, you might start to feel _____ .

A Surprise for Kate

Kate woke up and shouted,
"My birthday is here!
My classmates are coming.
I'm so full of cheer."

Kate searched for some presents.
She hoped for some skates.
"Guess Mom's still out shopping.
Why is she so late?"

Kate was in a sad state.
She raced to the den.
Why was there no cake there?
Frustrated again!

Kate cried to her father,
"You didn't decorate."
"My dear darling daughter,
You've got the wrong date."

Name: _____ **Date:** _____

A. Cross out the balloons that do <u>not</u> have the *–ate* word family. Color the balloons yellow that do have the *–ate* word family. Practice reading the *–ate* family words.

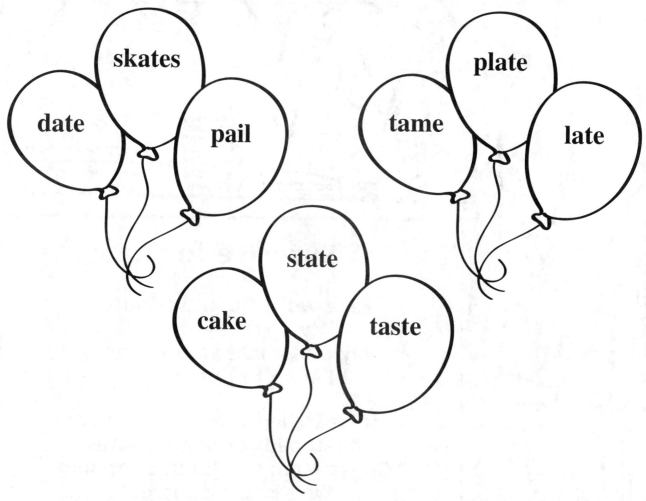

B. Use the balloons that have the *–ate* family words to fill in the blanks in the following sentences.

1. The _____ of my birthday is finally here!

2. I hope my friends will not be _____ .

3. One friend is coming from another _____ .

4. I hope I get a pair of _____ .

5. Put that cake right here on my _____ .

Name: _____ **Date:** _____

A. **Change the layers of the birthday cake by adding one new letter to each blank from the letter box.**

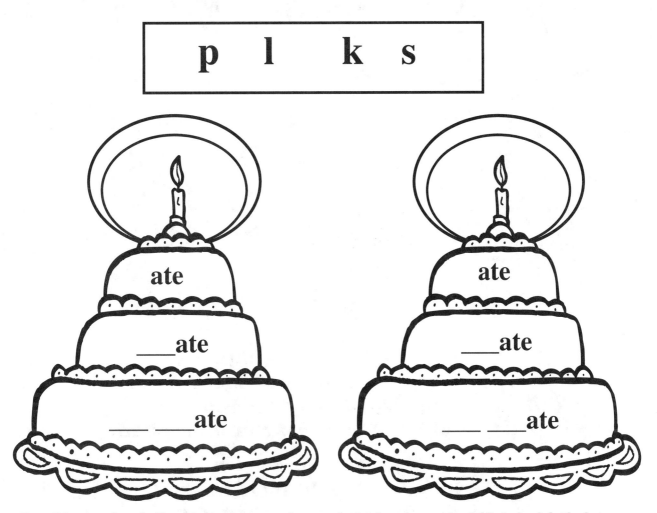

p	l	k	s

ate

___ate

___ ___ate

ate

___ate

___ ___ate

B. **Circle the following things that might be found at Kate's birthday party. Underline the *–ate* family words.**

classmates   a balloon to inflate

ice skates   a package to decorate

a shipmate   a piece of slate

cake on a plate   out-of-date toys

a painted gate   people to celebrate

Centipede's Vest of Tweed

Once there was a centipede,
That wore a handsome vest of tweed.
He had 100 legs indeed.
He thought that he could run with speed.

In the town of Tumbleweed,
A critter race would soon proceed.
The townsfolk bet on Centipede.
With all those legs, he would succeed.

Wise Owl attempted a good deed,
He said, "Some practice you will need.
And wear a jogging suit, take heed."
But Centipede was of a stubborn breed.

Centipede ran in his vest of tweed.
This didn't help him take the lead.
Hard work and practice he did need.
A lesson was learned by Centipede.

Name: _____ **Date:** _____

**A. Fill in the blanks with the *–eed* family word that makes sense.
Use the poem if you need help.**

1. Centipede looked good in his vest of _____ .

2. With all these legs, Centipede should _____ .

3. Wise owl tried to do a good _____ .

4. A jogging suit Centipede did _____ .

5. Centipede ran but didn't pick up _____ .

**B. You can help Centipede reach the finish line by following the
correct path. Draw a line to connect the sneakers that have an
–eed family word.**

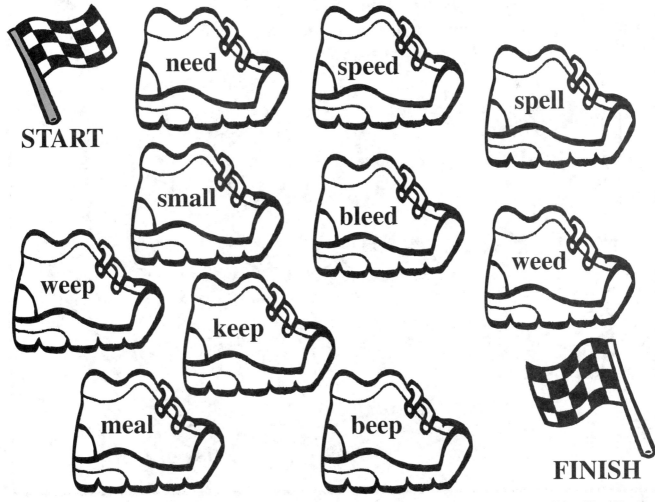

An Apple Fell

Right off a tree an apple fell.
Who should hit it?—Why, William Tell.
Swiftly his arrow did propel
And split that apple, so they tell.

Right off a tree an apple fell,
Where Isaac Newton sat a spell.
He had a thought clear as a bell
That gravity works very well.

Right off a tree an apple fell.
Johnny Appleseed cried, "That's really swell.
I'll plant apple seeds in the dell."
To friends and family he said, "Farewell."

Right off a tree an apple fell.
When it hit me, I surely did yell.
Then I smelled a heavenly smell
And ate that apple up, oh well!

Name: _____ **Date:** _____

A. Color the apples that make *–ell* family words red, yellow, or green.

B. Fill in the rhymes with an *–ell* family word.

Right off a tree an apple fell.
It hit a turtle on its _____ .

Do not eat the apple, Nell.
The wicked queen has cast a _____ .

Peter Pan heard a tiny yell.
Do you think it could be Tinker _____ ?

A huge apple in my yard fell.
I'll take it to school for show-and-_____ .

Name: _____ **Date:** _____

A. **Fill in the blanks using –***ell* **family words from the box below.**

smell	**spell**	**farewell**	**dwell**	**bell**

1. A worm might _____ inside an apple.

2. An apple pie has a wonderful _____ .

3. When the _____ rings, I'll bring an apple for my teacher.

4. Can you correctly _____ "applesauce"?

5. Now it is time to say "_____ ."

B. **Match the following people to what they might have said. Underline the –***ell* **family words.**

Johnny Appleseed

William Tell

Sir Isaac Newton

"Gravity has nothing to do with a magic spell."

"It would be swell if I could shoot this apple off my son's head."

"I'm off to plant apple trees. Farewell!"

A Whale's Trick

Just imagine watching whales
Aboard a ship that's quick.
We'd sail across the ocean blue
And never get seasick.

We'd listen very carefully,
For the whales' sounds click, click.
Perhaps we'd hear great big splashes
As the whales' tails flick.

They'd jump up very gracefully.
Their bodies are so slick.
If there's a great big monstrous one,
It might be Moby Dick.

With fascination we would stare.
They'd leap through waves so thick.
They'd splash water up on us.
Now that's a dirty trick!

Name: _____   **Date:** _____

A. How many whales will you see while whale watching? Circle the
whales that would make an *–ick* family word if *–ick* was added to their
waterspout. Practice reading the *–ick* family words.

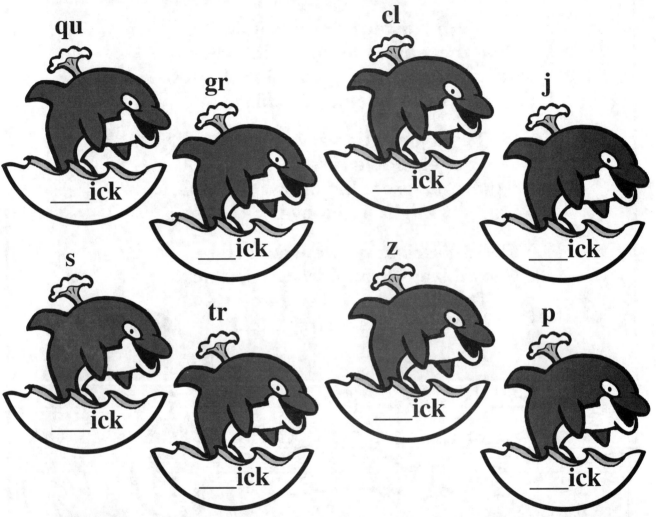

B. Fill in the sentences using *–ick* family words. Use the whales above
to help you.

1. We saw the whale do a neat _____ at
the show.
2. My camera went "_____" when I took
a picture.
3. The whale's _____ movement scared me.
4. _____ a good spot to stand on the
whale ship.
5. This ship is rocking. I feel _____!

Name: _____ **Date:** _____

A. Solve the *–ick* family word riddles about whales.

---

thick   seasick   sidekick   yardstick   slick

---

1. A buddy or close friend who might join you whale watching could be called your _____ .

2. A measuring device that is 36 inches long and is used to measure a whale's tail is a _____ .

3. The whale's body has a very _____ layer of blubber.

4. The motion of the boat while whale watching might make you feel dizzy and sick in your stomach. This is called being _____ .

5. The whale's body has a slippery smoothness. A word meaning a slippery smoothness is _____ .

B. Write "yes" or "no" to tell whether these sentences with *–ick* family words in them are real (yes) or make-believe (no). Circle all the *–ick* family words.

1. A trick that whales can be taught to do is to jump through a hoop. _____

2. A trick whales can be taught to do is to ride a broomstick.
_____

Bill and Jill

Two little ants named Bill and Jill
Lived in the park in their anthill.

Each morning at precisely six,
They'd climb their hill with skis and sticks.

All summer long they'd practice drills
So that in winter they'd have skills.

While other ants were lying still,
Sleeping throughout the winter chill,

Ants Bill and Jill enjoyed the thrill
Of skiing down their icy hill.

Sometimes there'd be a sound so shrill
As one of them did take a spill.

I know someday that there will be
Olympic gold for ants that ski.

Name: _____ **Date:** _____

A. **Make a word by putting together the *–ill* family word sounds going down the anthills. Write the word when you reach the bottom.**

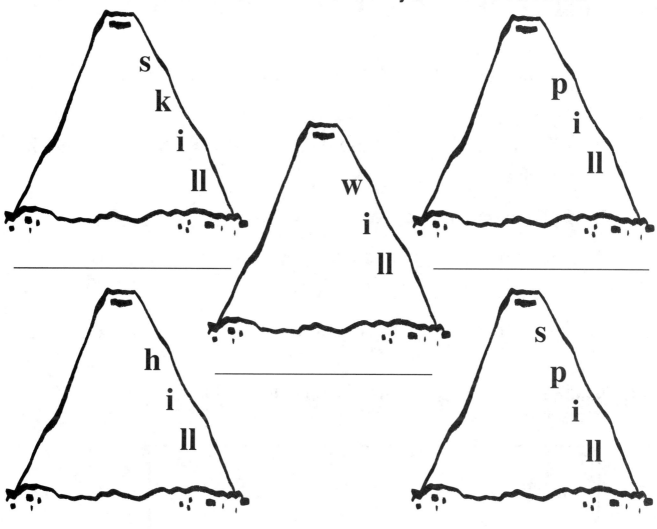

B. **Use the words from above in the sentences below.**

1. Skiing takes a lot of _____ .

2. I like to go up to the highest _____ .

3. Once I hit a bump and took a bad _____ .

4. The doctor told me, "Please take this _____ ."

5. I told the doctor, "Yes, I _____ ."

Name: _____ **Date:** _____

A. **Answer the following riddles with an *–ill* family word. Change a letter or add a letter from the prior riddle to create the answer to the new riddle.**

1. This is a landform similar to a mountain but smaller:

   _____ .

2. A flat piece of wood at the bottom of the window frame is

   called a _____ .

3. If you practice hard, you will have a _____ .

4. Liquid that pours out accidentally from a container is a

   _____ .

5. If something is not moving, it is very _____ .

B. **Match each word part with an *–ill* family word to make a compound word.**

window	mill
ant	sill
good	hill
wind	still
stand	will

Sing, Sing, Sing!

What joy it brings for me to sing.
I sing about most anything.

I sing in summer and in spring.
I sit and sing on my porch swing.

If the phone rings, ding-a-ling,
I sing hello into that thing.

My teacher wrings her hands at school.
She warns, "Don't sing, follow the rule."

My sister flings her arms at me.
She cries, "Stop singing, you're off-key."

My mother tries to make me stop.
She brings to me a lollipop.

But, I care little of their sneers,
For I've got cotton in my ears.

Name: _____ **Date:** _____

A. **If the girl in the poem only sang songs with an *–ing* family word in the title, which songs would she sing? Write "yes" or "no" on the lines.**

1. "Spring Has Sprung"   5. "A Bee Sting"

   _____   _____

2. "Summer Time"   6. "Pretty Flowers"

   _____   _____

3. "The King's Crown"   7. "Snow Day"

   _____   _____

4. "A Sparkling Ring"   8. "On a Swing"

   _____   _____

B. **Use the letter tiles to build some *–ing* family words.**

s   p   r   t   k   w

1. ____ ing   5. ____ ing

2. ____ ing   6. ____ ____ ing

3. ____ ing   7. ____ ____ ing

4. ____ ing   8. ____ ____ ____ ing

Name: _____ **Date:** _____

A. Find out what the girl in the poem is singing about from these song lyrics. Use the *–ing* family words from the box below to help you.

| spring   king   sling   swing   ring |
---

1.   He wears a crown upon his head.
      He is a man who is well-bred.

      _____

2.   It is what's left when you empty the tub.
      To get it off you have to rub.

      _____

3.   I fell and caused myself some harm.
      I have to wear this on my arm.

      _____

4.   I play on this at the playground.
      With one good push, I'm upward bound.

      _____

5.   My pogo stick has this inside.
      I jump so high, I'm terrified!

      _____

B. Make compound words containing *–ing*. Draw lines to match. One word on the right will have more than one match.

---
any

ear   thing

some   ring

every

Madge, the Mink

Madge Mink squeaked to Sally Skunk
While on the brink of war,
"I protect my babies best
Because my stink smells more."

Hungry fox was listening,
And he began to think.
A sneaky plan popped in his head,
And he was tickled pink.

"Over yonder is a tree.
Stand by it, you fine ladies.
Let out your scent and I will judge."
He then winked at their babies.

Madge Mink slinked up to the tree.
Sly fox crept to their nests.
Sally shouted, "Stop, you fink!"
And sprayed him on his chest.

Madge, the mink, rethinking said,
"As friends we're linked forever.
You saved the day and you have won
Because you are so clever!"

INK Word Family _Madge, the Mink_

Name: _____ Date: _____

A. In the poem, Madge and Sally were enemies and then friends. Read the sentences containing _–ink_ family words. Draw a happy face on the line if it is a friendly thing for someone to say. Draw a sad face if it is not. Underline the _–ink_ family words.

1. I like your pink dress. _____

2. I won't go to the roller rink with you! _____

3. That's not right! What were you thinking? _____

4. May I get a drink of water? _____

5. You may use my ink pen. _____

B. Draw a picture to illustrate the following sentences. Underline the _–ink_ family words.

1. I got a drink of water from the sink.

2. I think I smell a stinky skunk.

©*Teacher Created Resources, Inc.*   33   *#8978 Phonics Poetry Using Word Families*

A Goat's Float

In the field stood Betty Goat
Wearing a hot pink petticoat.
Across the lake was Billy Goat.
She saw he had two root beer floats.

Betty stopped munching on her oats.
She grabbed her yellow overcoat.
She climbed aboard an old rowboat
And headed off toward Billy Goat.

A storm came up and rocked the boat.
How would Betty Goat stay afloat?
She made some sails with her overcoat
As well as with her petticoat.

Soon the two goats sipped root beer floats.
Then Betty began to clear her throat.
She said, "I really hate to gloat,
But I'm a mighty good sailing goat."

Name: _____ **Date:** _____

A. **Color the floats that help make the** *–oat* **family words. Write the words on the line below the picture. Practice reading the words.**

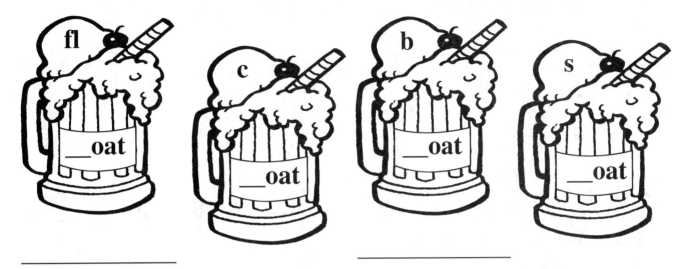

_____   _____

_____   _____

_____   _____   _____

B. **Fill in the blanks with the** *–oat* **family words from above.**

1. Betty, the _____ , was eating her oats.

2. Billy, the goat, had a root beer _____ .

3. Betty put on her yellow _____ .

4. She hopped onto a small _____ .

5. She said, "I do not like to _____ ."

Name: _____ Date: _____

A. Use the *–oat* family words found in the word box below to complete the crossword puzzle.

Across

4. A hoofed animal
5. A part of your neck
7. Heavy coat worn over your clothing
8. A grain used for food

Down

1. To stay on the surface of the water
2. A fancy skirt with lace or ruffles
3. A small boat with oars
6. Feeling great pride

throat	oat	overcoat	float	gloat
petticoat		goat		rowboat

B. Betty was proud of herself and was gloating. Tell about a time that you felt proud and wanted to gloat.

_____

_____

Paul, the Peacock

Paul, the proud peacock, had a musical dream,
To be a rock star and make peahens scream.

With his tail unfurled, he'd strut around the block.
When everyone saw him, they'd go into shock.

He'd strum his guitar by the dock on a stage.
He hoped that his music would be all the rage.

But, what was that noise, that horrible squawk?
It was the terrible vocals of Paul, the peacock.

Poor Paul, the peacock, the people did mock.
This once proud peacock was a big laughingstock.

Is Paul's dream now over? No, hens come in flocks,
For Paul stopped his singing, but his guitar still rocks.

Name: _____ **Date:** _____

A. **Use yellow to color feathers whose letters will help make an *–ock* family word. Color the other feathers different colors.**

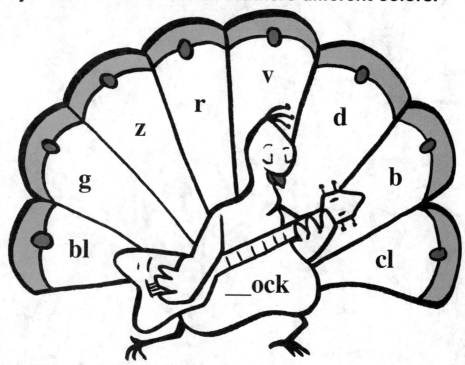

B. **Make new words by adding and changing letters. Practice reading the words.**

1. I am a dock.

    d _____ o _____ c _____ k _____

2. Change my first letter to a "l."

    _____ _____ _____ _____

3. Add a "b" before the "l."

    _____ _____ _____ _____ _____

4. Change my first letter to an "f."

    _____ _____ _____ _____

5. Change my first letter to a "c."

    _____ _____ _____ _____

The Drop of Three Eggs

Upon the floor three eggs did drop,
Plop, Plop, Plop!

Poor doggie slid and could not stop,
Flop, Flop, Flop!

Quick, Mama, go and grab the mop,
Slop, Slop, Slop!

Please get more eggs now, our dear Pop,
Shop, Shop, Shop!

Name: _____ **Date:** _____

A. **Color the eggs that would make an *–op* family word when the two halves are put back together.**

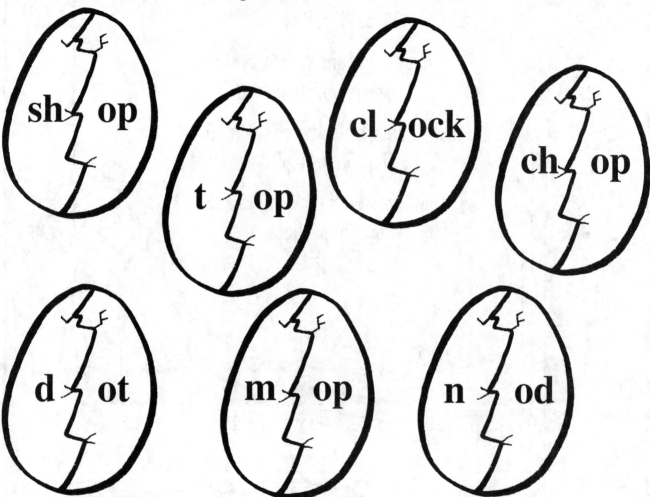

B. **Use the poem "The Drop of Three Eggs" to fill in the correct *–op* family word.**

1. When the eggs fell, they made the sound _____ .

2. When the doggie slid, he made the sound _____ .

3. When Mama mopped up the spill, it made the sound

   _____ .

4. To get new eggs, Pop went to the store to _____ .

5. Pop hopes that no more eggs will _____ .

Just My Luck

I found a shiny penny.
I was sure it would bring luck.
But this story is a sad one,
For not good but bad luck struck.

When I awoke next morning
To my pillow I was stuck,
For the gum I had been chewing
Found its way to my hair—Yuck!

I tried to take a warm bath
With my little rubber duck.
But my older brother took it
To use for a hockey puck.

I wanted to play outside
With my good ol' pal Chucky,
But he went to see his grandma.
I think she's in Kentucky.

So I took that lucky penny,
And I chucked it in the muck.
And if I see another one—
Shucks, it might bring me luck.

Name: _____ **Date:** _____

A. **Find and list all the _–uck_ family words in the poem. Do not use the same word more than once. Practice reading the words.**

1. _____   7. _____

2. _____   8. _____

3. _____   9. _____

4. _____   10. _____

5. _____   11. _____

6. _____   12. _____

B. **Circle the pennies that you would consider to be unlucky ones.**

After I found this penny . . .

1.
our car needed
a tow truck.

2.
my hockey puck
went in the goal.

3.
I struck out at my
baseball game.

4.
I won a yellow
duck at the fair.

5.
I got stuck on a
math problem.

6.
I got five bucks for
doing my chores.

Name: _____ **Date:** _____

A. Use the words from the box below to fill in the blanks.

stuck	Kentucky	Duck	starstruck
luck	knuckles	pluck	dumbstruck

My Lucky Day

One day my mother took me to a concert in

_____ . I was _____ by the

performers. I wanted to be just like them. What

_____ ! They were asking for volunteers to

come up and sing. I _____ my hand right up.

The guitar player started to _____. I opened

my mouth but nothing came out. I was _____ .

My _____ were turning white. Luckily, my

fear soon passed. I think I sounded just like Donald

_____ , but I did it!

B. Tell about a time when you had good luck. Use some *–uck* family words in your story.

_____

_____

_____

_____

Busy Bug

Where have you been, busy bug, busy bug?
I've been hiding under the rug,
SNUG, SNUG, SNUG!

Where have you been, busy bug, busy bug?
Drinking lemonade from a mug,
GLUG, GLUG, GLUG!

Where have you been, busy bug, busy bug?
Riding on a locomotive,
CHUG, CHUG, CHUG!

Where have you been , busy bug, busy bug?
I've been dancing with ladybug,
JITTERBUG, JITTERBUG!

It's time for bed, busy bug, busy bug!
So say good-night to Mama and
HUG, HUG, HUG!

44 ©Teacher Created Resources, Inc.

Name: _____ Date: _____

A. Find and list all the *–ug* family words in the poem. Do not use the same word more than once. Practice reading the words.

1. _____   6. _____

2. _____   7. _____

3. _____   8. _____

4. _____   9. _____

5. _____

B. Write a story about a bug. Make sure to use some *–ug* family words in your story.

_____

_____

_____

_____

_____

_____

_____

Name: _____ Date: _____

A. Fill in the web to tell what things Busy Bug did during his busy day.

B. Use –*ug* family words to complete the blanks below.

hug	rug	mug	slug	plug

1. Busy Bug made lots of noise when he did the jitterbug.
   Mama had to _____ her ears.

2. Busy Bug asked Mama, "Can I please have a drink of
   water in my _____ ?"

3. Mama bought a new _____ for the floor in
   Busy Bug's bedroom.

4. One day Busy Bug played with a slimy _____ .

5. Don't forget to give Mama a kiss and a _____ .

Answer Key

Page 5

A. The following footballs should be colored: bl, qu, sn, tr, j. The boxes should be filled in as follows: black, jacks, quack, track, snack.

B.
1. track
2. snack
3. quack
4. black
5. jacks

Page 6

A. lumberjack, haystack, icepack, quarterback, racetrack

B.
1. yes   6. yes
2. no   7. no
3. yes   8. yes
4. no   9. no
5. yes   10. no

Page 8

A. The following gumballs should be colored: c (call), st (stall), b (ball), sm (small), f (fall), w (wall).

B.
1. mall
2. Call
3. small
4. fall
5. ball

Page 10

A.
1. clam
2. Birmingham
3. swam
4. Pam
5. exam
6. cram
7. Sam
8. jam
9. Wham
10. slammed
11. scram
12. am

B. The following clams should be colored: ham, jam, yam, ram. The following clams should be crossed out: gam, nam, xam.

Page 11

A. jam, slam, clammy, Wham, scram

B. Students should describe a time that they were in trouble. Answers will vary.

Page 13

A. The following fish should be circled: thank, bank, tank, sank, clank.

B.
1. bank
2. tank
3. sank
4. clank
5. Thank

Page 14

A. The following bubbles should be colored: cl (clank), bl (blank), th (thank), dr (drank), shr (shrank).

B.
1. plank
2. blank
3. outranks
4. yank
5. cranky

Page 16

A. The following balloons should be crossed out: pail, cake, taste, tame.

B.
1. date
2. late
3. state
4. skates
5. plate

Page 17

A. late, plate, Kate, skate

B. The following should be circled: classmates, ice skates, cake on a plate, a balloon to inflate, a package to decorate, people to celebrate.
The following words should be underlined: classmates, skates, shipmate, plate, gate, inflate, decorate, slate, out-of-date, celebrate.

Page 19

A.
1. tweed
2. succeed
3. deed
4. need
5. speed

B. The following shoes need to be connected: need, speed, bleed, weed.

Page 21

A. The following apples should be colored: sell, tell, yell, well.

B. shell, spell, Bell, tell

Page 22

A.
1. dwell
2. smell
3. bell
4. spell
5. farewell

B. *Johnny Appleseed:* "I'm off to plant apple trees, farewell!"

William Tell: "It would be swell if I could shoot this apple off my son's head."

Sir Isaac Newton: "Gravity has nothing to do with a magic spell."

Page 24

A. quick, click, sick, trick, pick

B.
1. trick
2. click
3. quick
4. Pick
5. sick

Page 25

A.
1. sidekick
2. yardstick
3. thick
4. seasick
5. slick

B.
1. yes
2. no
The following words should be circled: trick, trick, broomstick.

Answer Key

Page 27

A. skill, will, pill, hill, spill

B. 1. skill
   2. hill
   3. spill
   4. pill
   5. will

Page 28

A. 1. hill
   2. sill
   3. skill
   4. spill
   5. still

B. windowsill
   anthill
   goodwill
   windmill
   standstill

Page 30

A. 1. yes   5. yes
   2. no   6. no
   3. yes   7. no
   4. yes   8. yes

B. The following are words
   that could be made: sing,
   ring, king, wing, ping, sting,
   swing, spring.

Page 31

A. 1. king
   2. ring
   3. sling
   4. swing
   5. spring

B. anything
   earring
   something
   everything

Page 33

A. 1. happy face
   2. sad face
   3. sad face
   4. happy face
   5. happy face
   Words that need to be
   underlined: pink, rink,
   thinking, drink, ink.

B. Appropriate illustrations
   should be provided. The
   following words should be
   underlined: drink, sink,
   think, stinky.

Page 35

A. The following floats should
   be colored: float, coat, boat,
   goat, gloat.

B. 1. goat
   2. float
   3. coat
   4. boat
   5. gloat

Page 36

A. *Across*
   4. goat
   5. throat
   7. overcoat
   8. oat
   Down
   1. float
   2. petticoat
   3. rowboat
   6. gloat

B. Answers will vary. They
   should tell about a time
   when the student felt proud.

Page 38

A. The following feathers
   should be colored yellow:
   bl (block), r (rock),
   d (dock), cl (clock).

B. 1. dock
   2. lock
   3. block
   4. flock
   5. clock

Page 40

A. The following eggs should be
   colored: shop, top, chop, mop.

B. 1. plop
   2. flop
   3. slop
   4. shop
   5. drop

Page 42

A. 1. luck
   2. struck
   3. stuck
   4. Yuck
   5. duck
   6. puck
   7. Chucky
   8. Kentucky
   9. lucky
   10. chucked
   11. muck
   12. shucks

B. The following pennies
   should be circled: 1, 3, 5.

Page 43

A. Kentucky, starstruck, luck,
   stuck, pluck, dumbstruck,
   knuckles, Duck

B. Answers will vary. A
   good luck story should be
   provided.

Page 45

A. 1. bug
   2. rug
   3. snug
   4. mug
   5. glug
   6. chug
   7. ladybug
   8. jitterbug
   9. hug

B. Stories should include –ug
   family words.

Page 46

A. hid under a rug, drank
   lemonade, rode a locomotive,
   danced, went to bed

B. 1. plug
   2. mug
   3. rug
   4. slug
   5. hug